Jane Bingham

Published in 2013 by Wayland

Copyright © Wayland 2013

Wayland
338 Euston Road
London NW1 3BH

Wayland Australia
Level 17/207 Kent Street
Sydney NSW 2000

Editor: Katie Powell
Designer: Phipps Design
Picture Researcher: Shelley Noronha

British Library Cataloguing in Publication Data

Bingham, Jane.
Henry VIII. – (Extraordinary lives)
1.Henry VIII,King of England, 1491-1547–Juvenile literature.
2.Great Britain–Kings and rulers–Biography–Juvenile literature.
3.Great Britain–History–Henry VIII, 1509-1547–Juvenile literature.
I.Title II. Series
942'.052'092-dc22

ISBN: 978 0 7502 7952 9

10 9 8 7 6 5 4 3 2 1

Picture acknowledgements: cover VIII © Walker Art Gallery,National Museums Liverpool/ The Bridgeman Art Library, p4 © The Art Archive / Musée du Château de Versailles / Gianni Dagli Orti, p5 © Walker Art Gallery,National Museums Liverpool / The Bridgeman Art Library, p6 © The Berger Collection at the Denver Art Museum,USA / The Bridgeman Art Library, p7 © 2003 Topham Picturepoint, p8 © Musee des Gobelins, Paris, France / Lauros / Giraudon/ The Bridgeman Art Library, p9 © Hatfield House,Hertfordshire, UK / The Bridgeman Art Library, p10 © Istock, p11 © The Granger Collection /TopFoto, p12 ©Mary Evans Picture Library, p13 © Hever Castle,Kent, UK/ The Bridgeman Art Library, p14 © iStock, p15 © iStock, p16 © Kunsthistorisches Museum,Vienna,Austria / The Bridgeman Art Library, p17 © Wayland (NPG), p18 © The Art Archive / Musée du Louvre Paris / Gianni Dagli Orti, p19 © The Trustees of the Weston Park Foundation,UK / The Bridgeman Art Library, p20 © Mary Evans Picture Library, p21 © The Barnes Foundation, Merion, Pennsylvania,USA / The Bridgeman Art Library, p22 © Private Collection/ The Bridgeman Art Library, p23 © The Art Archive / Private Collection Italy / Gianni Dagli Orti, p24 © Wayland(NPG), p25 © The Art Archive / Galleria degli Uffizi Florence / Gianni Dagli Orti, p26 © Getty Images, p27 © Wayland (NPG)

Every effort has been made to clear copyright. Should there be any inadvertent omission, please apply to the publisher for rectification.

Printed in China

Wayland is a division of Hachette Children's Books, an Hachette UK company.
www.hachette.co.uk

Contents

Words that appear in **bold** can be
found in the glossary.

Henry VIII – an extraordinary king

I n May 1520, **a fleet** of ships set sail from Dover. In the leading ship was the young King Henry VIII. On the shore, the crowds cheered wildly for their king. He was clever, handsome and confident – and he made them feel proud to be English.

The Field of the Cloth of Gold

King Henry and his court were heading for a meeting with the King of France. After years of fighting, the two kings were signing a peace **treaty**. The meeting was also a great chance for Henry to show off.

This painting shows Henry riding to meet the French King at the Field of the Cloth of Gold in France.

In a large field in northern France, the French and English courts set up amazing 'cities' made from golden tents. For the next two weeks, they held a non-stop party. The two young kings rivalled each other in **jousting**, singing and making speeches. It was one of the high points of Henry's **reign**.

A dramatic reign

Henry ruled England for 38 years, from 1509 to 1547. In that period, he created an independent English Church, fought off **invasions**, and made his country feared and respected. He also got married six times!

Henry VIII had his faults – he had a violent temper and he sometimes treated his enemies brutally. But he was a remarkable king who inspired feelings of awe and pride in his people.

Henry VIII was a larger-than-life character. This famous portrait is by Hans Holbein.

A TUDOR KING

Henry VIII belonged to the Tudor family, who ruled England for over a hundred years. Altogether, there were five Tudor monarchs:

Henry VII   1485–1509
Henry VIII   1509–1547
Edward VI   1547–1553
Mary I   1553–1558
Elizabeth I   1558–1603

Prince Henry

On 28 June 1491, a prince was born in the royal palace at Greenwich, in London. He was the second son of King Henry VII, and he was given his father's name. Prince Henry grew up to be strong, handsome and clever, but he had a fiery temper.

Lessons and fun

Prince Henry had all his lessons at home in the royal palace. His tutor was the poet John Skelton and he taught Henry **theology**, Latin and Greek. Henry was good at all his lessons, but he liked music and poetry most of all.

A portrait of Henry as a young man. Even when he was young, he had a very strong character.

Henry loved to spend time out of doors. Whenever he could, he went riding and hunting. He also played an early form of tennis known as 'real tennis'.

'Real tennis' was played in a court with very high walls. Henry had a tennis court built for him at his palace at Hampton Court.

Preparing to rule

When Henry was 10 years old, his older brother, Arthur, died. Overnight, Henry became the **heir** to the English throne. Prince Arthur was 16 when he died, but he was already married to Catherine of Aragon, the daughter of the King of Spain. After Arthur's death, Henry had to agree that he would marry Catherine when he was older. Spain was a powerful country and it was very important that England and Spain remained **allies**.

DYING YOUNG

Prince Arthur's death was not unusual. In Tudor times, six out of 10 children never reached their twenties. Henry had six brothers and sisters, but only two of them (Margaret and Mary) survived into adult life.

Long live the King!

King Henry VII died when Prince Henry was 17 years old. The new king was crowned in June 1509, and six weeks later he married Catherine of Aragon, who was then aged 23. Henry held lavish parties to celebrate the beginning of his reign.

A fresh start

Henry wanted to prove that he was very different from his father. He knew that the English people hated his father's tax collectors so he gave orders for the two leading collectors to be executed. However, Henry VIII still collected **taxes** from his subjects.

The young king also invited poets, artists and musicians to perform at the royal court. Henry's splendid court was famous throughout Europe, but it was very expensive to run.

This tapestry shows the kind of life that Henry enjoyed – filled with music and dancing.

RICH AND POOR IN TUDOR TIMES

Royalty and **nobles** lived in beautiful houses with enormous grounds and had many servants to look after them. Their children were taught by private tutors and they enjoyed music and dancing, **falconry** and hunting. The rich ate plenty of meat and fish, and held grand banquets with many courses, washed down with fine French wine.

Poor people in Tudor times had a very hard life. In the country, they worked as servants or as farm workers and even the children were expected to work hard. Most of their meals were bread and soup. Meat was a luxury but some people kept animals to provide them with milk, cheese and eggs. Poor people in towns worked as craftworkers or shopkeepers. They lived in narrow, crowded streets with no proper drains.

This painting shows a Tudor fair. The rich visitors to the fair are dressed in the latest fashions. The poor people wear ragged clothes and work as servants.

Wars and disagreements

At the start of his reign, Henry faced danger from several directions. France was an old enemy and the King of Scotland was also a threat. Henry was determined to show his enemies that England was a country to be feared.

Henry's wars

In 1513, Henry led an army across the English Channel to fight against France. After a short struggle, he won the Battle of Spurs. Henry had proved himself a strong war leader, but there was bad news from home. While he was away the Scots had marched south into England.

Following Henry's orders, an English army attacked the Scots and defeated them at the Battle of Flodden. The Scottish king was killed and his troops retreated. After Flodden, Scotland was no longer a threat to Henry – until the last years of his reign.

Henry owned over 60 houses and palaces but Hampton Court was the grandest.

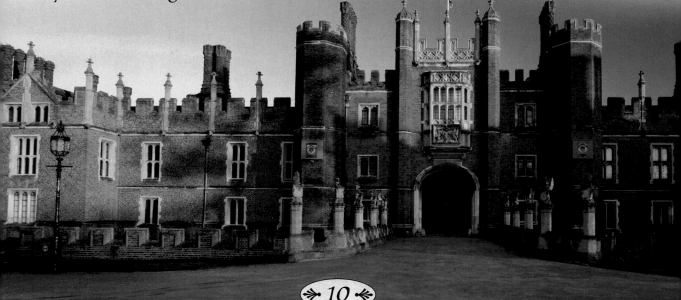

Henry's advisors

Henry wasn't interested in the details of running his country. Instead, he chose some powerful advisors to help him make decisions. In the early part of his reign, he relied mainly on Thomas Wolsey.

This Tudor painting shows King Henry jousting, while his wife, Catherine of Aragon, watches the tournament. Henry has just broken his lance!

In 1515, Henry made Wolsey his chancellor, putting him in charge of the royal fortunes. Wolsey used some of this money to build himself an enormous palace at Hampton Court. This made Henry so jealous that he forced Wolsey to give him the palace as a present!

PRACTISING FOR WAR

Henry loved to take part in tournaments. These were mock battles in which two men in armour charged at each other on horseback. Nobody could tell who was inside the armour. Sometimes, Henry would only reveal who he was after he had won a victory!

Catherine and Anne

In 1516, Henry's wife, Catherine of Aragon, gave birth to a daughter, Mary. Henry thought he would soon have a son, but all Catherine's other babies died at birth. Henry believed that only a man could rule England, so he was desperate for a son and heir.

Catherine of Aragon was an intelligent woman and a member of the Roman Catholic Church.

Henry and Anne

By 1527, Henry and Catherine had been married for 18 years and they still had only one daughter.

PRINCESS MARY

Henry's daughter Mary is often known as Mary Tudor. She grew up to be a keen **Roman Catholic**, like her mother. Mary was Queen of England from 1553 to 1558. During her reign, she gave orders for many **Protestants** to be executed, and gained the nickname 'Bloody Mary'.

Henry began to think that God was punishing him for marrying his brother's wife. At the same time, he had fallen in love with Anne Boleyn, one of the ladies-in-waiting at the royal court. He made up his mind to leave Catherine and marry Anne.

Problems with the Pope

Before Henry could marry again, he needed permission from the **Pope** – the head of the Roman Catholic Church. He asked the Pope to declare that his marriage to Catherine was unlawful, because he had married his brother's wife. When the Pope refused, Henry was furious. He blamed Thomas Wolsey for siding with the Pope, and had him arrested for **treason**.

Henry's new advisor, Thomas Cromwell, gave him some bold advice. He said that Henry must break away completely from the Pope and the Roman Catholic Church.

Anne Boleyn had many admirers. People described her eyes as 'black and beautiful'.

Head of the Church

In 1533, Henry broke away from the Roman Catholic Church. This meant he could divorce Catherine. Then, in 1534, he declared himself Supreme Head of the Church in England. Henry's dramatic move also created an independent English Church.

Wealth from monasteries

Two years after Henry's break from Rome, he decided to close down England's monasteries. He claimed that the monks and nuns were no longer leading holy lives. This was partly true, because there were many problems in the Catholic Church. However, Henry really wanted more money and land. He was running out of funds and the monasteries were very rich.

Fountains Abbey in Yorkshire was one of many monasteries left to fall into ruins after Thomas Cromwell's raids.

Thomas Cromwell's men drove the monks and nuns out of their homes, and seized their land and treasures for the king. The monks and nuns were left homeless, and the monasteries fell into poor condition.

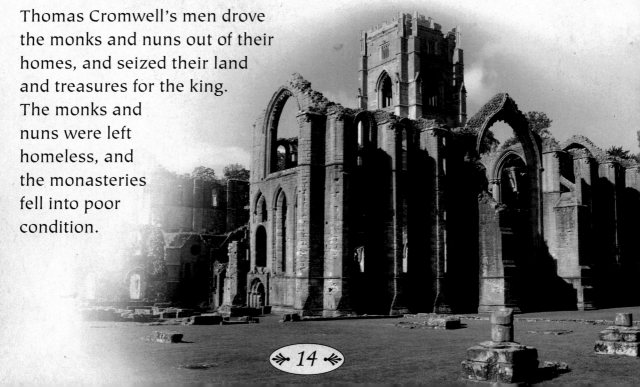

CATHOLICS AND PROTESTANTS

Henry VIII was not the first to break away from the Roman Catholic Church. In 1517, a German monk called Martin Luther protested against the way the Catholic Church was run. Luther wanted a simpler form of worship, based on the teachings of the Bible.

By the 1530s, people all over Germany were holding simple services following Luther's ideas. This was the start of the Protestant movement. Europe became split between Catholics and Protestants, and the Protestant movement was especially strong in Germany.

Members of Henry's Church of England were known as Protestants, because they had broken away from the Pope. But, in fact, the Church of England was not like the rest of the Protestant movement and Henry strongly disapproved of Luther's views.

This statue shows Martin Luther, the founder of the Protestant movement, holding a copy of the Bible.

Weddings, births and deaths

Henry married Anne Boleyn in 1533. Later that year, Anne gave birth to a daughter, Elizabeth. Henry had planned a big party to celebrate the birth of his son, but when Elizabeth was born he cancelled all his plans.

The end of Anne

In the following year, Anne had a second child – a boy who was born dead. By this time, Henry was tired of his wife's hot temper and he wanted to get rid of her. He accused Anne of having love affairs with other men and gave orders that she should be tried for treason against the king. She was found guilty and beheaded in 1536.

Henry and Jane

Just two weeks after Anne's death, Henry married again. His third wife was Jane Seymour, one of Anne's ladies-in-waiting.

Jane Seymour came from a noble family, but unlike Henry's first two wives, she was not very well educated.

Jane was quiet and gentle, unlike the fiery Anne. She banned the fancy French fashions that Anne had introduced into the royal court. She also encouraged Henry to be kinder to his daughter, Mary.

In 1537, Jane gave birth to a son, named Edward, but she died 12 days later. Henry was heartbroken, but he had an heir at last.

PRINCE EDWARD

Prince Edward was a lively, intelligent boy. He became king at the age of nine, but his uncle, Edward Seymour, took charge of the business of ruling the country. Edward never had the chance to reign on his own. He died from tuberculosis (a serious lung disease) at the age of 15.

When Henry VIII died in 1547, his only son was crowned King Edward VI. Edward was king for just six years, until his early death in 1553.

A German wife

After Jane Seymour's death, Henry stayed single for three years. Then Thomas Cromwell suggested that Henry should marry Anne of Cleves, a German princess. Germany was a powerful Protestant country. If Henry married Anne, England and Germany would become allies.

A very short marriage

Henry sent the artist Hans Holbein to paint a portrait of Anne of Cleves. Henry admired the portrait, but when Anne came to England he was disappointed. He rudely said she looked like a horse.

Hans Holbein painted this portrait of Anne of Cleves so that Henry VIII could see what she looked like. Henry wanted a realistic portrait of his future wife.

 THE KING'S PAINTER

Holbein was a German artist who became the King's Painter in 1535. Henry greatly admired Holbein's skill. He once told a nobleman, 'Of seven peasants I can make seven lords, but not one Holbein'.

The wedding went ahead, but after six months Henry sent Anne away, saying she did not please him. Their marriage was **annulled** and Anne lived quietly in the country for the rest of her life. She stayed good friends with Henry, who gave her the title 'the King's beloved sister'.

Losing advisors

Henry was worried that his failed marriage had made him look stupid. He hated being laughed at and he blamed the disaster on his advisor, Cromwell. Henry became more and more suspicious of Cromwell. In 1540, he gave orders that Cromwell should be arrested and beheaded without a trial.

Cromwell was not the first advisor who Henry had put to death. Five years earlier, Sir Thomas More had refused to side with the king in his quarrel with the Pope. Even though More was an old friend of Henry's, he too was tried for treason and beheaded.

Thomas Cromwell was King Henry VIII's chief minister and advisor for eight years, from 1532 to 1540. This portrait of Cromwell was painted by Hans Holbein.

Henry's troubles grow

Henry felt very lonely after Cromwell's death. He no longer had any advisors he could trust, and he was starting to feel old and ill. Henry had given up horse riding after a bad fall and had become extremely fat. His temper had grown worse and everyone at court was frightened of him.

A young wife

In 1540, Henry married Catherine Howard. He was 49, and she was only 19. Henry hoped that his new young wife would make him happy, but Catherine was soon flirting with other men. Henry was furious and he gave orders that she should be tried for treason. Less than two years after her marriage to the king, Catherine was beheaded.

Catherine Howard was pretty and lively. She found her husband unattractive and encouraged her many admirers at court.

TUDOR PUNISHMENTS

During the course of his reign, Henry ordered many executions – especially for people who he believed had betrayed him. These orders were cruel and violent, but execution was not unusual in Tudor times. More than 70,000 people were executed during Henry's reign.

In Tudor times, people believed that punishments should be very frightening, so that nobody would dare to break the law. People were put to death for treason and murder, but also for **rioting** and stealing. Nobles were usually beheaded on a block, while poor people were hung from a **gallows**.

Minor punishments included being whipped in public, being burned with a red-hot iron, and being held in the stocks (see picture below).

A Tudor painting of two men locked in the stocks. The man on the left is a poor criminal. The one on the right is a wealthy man, who is being visited by a friend.

Defending England

In the last years of his reign, Henry fought the Scots once again. This time he defeated them at the Battle of Solway Moss in 1542. He also faced more threats from the King of France, who had plans to invade England.

Keeping safe

Fortunately, Henry was ready to fight off invaders. Over the years, he had created a powerful **navy**. He had also built a series of forts along the south coast.

This painting shows the *Mary Rose*, one of Henry VIII's favourite ships. The remains of the ship were rescued in 1982.

In 1545, over 200 French ships launched their attack. The English fleet sailed towards them, firing their cannons, and the French retreated. The English had triumphed, but there was one terrible loss. As Henry watched from the shore, one of his finest ships, the *Mary Rose*, rolled over and sank.

THE RENAISSANCE WORLD

Henry VIII ruled England at a very exciting time. In the 1450s, a movement called the **Renaissance** had begun in Italy. During the Renaissance, people rediscovered the art and ideas of ancient Greece and Rome. Many great artists and thinkers lived in Europe during this period.

Henry's reign was also a time of exploration and discovery. Christopher Columbus had reached America in 1492, the year after Henry was born. During Henry's reign, the Spanish and Portuguese established thriving **colonies** in South America. In 1522, when Henry was 31, Ferdinand Magellan's ship sailed all the way round the world.

Around the year 1450, Johannnes Gutenberg invented the printing press in Germany. By the start of Henry's reign in 1509, printed books were being produced all over Europe.

In the early years of Henry VIII's reign, the great artist and inventor Leonardo da Vinci was working in Italy. This is a self-portrait by Leonardo.

Henry's last years

In 1543, Henry married his sixth wife, Catherine Parr. He was 52, but he seemed like an old man. He had poisonous **ulcers** on his legs, which smelled disgusting. He couldn't walk without help and he suffered from raging headaches. He also believed that people at court were plotting to kill him.

Catherine and Henry

Catherine Parr put up with Henry's bad temper, and nursed him patiently as he grew weaker. Elizabeth and Edward were nine and five at the time of her marriage, and Catherine made sure that they had an excellent education.

Catherine Parr married again after Henry's death. In 1548, she had a daughter, but she died six days after her daughter's birth.

By the end of his life, Henry was very bad tempered and most people were afraid of him.

Death of a king

Henry died in his royal palace at Whitehall at the age of 55. He was buried in St. George's Chapel, Windsor, next to the grave of his third wife, Jane Seymour. After Henry's death, nine year old Edward became king, but he only lived for six more years. Then Mary reigned until her death five years later, in 1558. Finally, Elizabeth I came to the throne and was queen for the next 45 years (1558–1603).

KING-SIZED MONARCH

Henry loved to dress up in armour for special occasions, such as tournaments. His suits of armour were specially made for him, and they were enormous. One of his last suits had a waist measuring 132 centimetres (52 inches)!

Why is Henry VIII important today?

Henry VIII is famous today for his six wives and for his larger-than-life personality. But he also made important changes in English society. Some of Henry's changes had a permanent effect on life in England.

Changes in England

After Henry's quarrel with the Pope, he became the head of the English Church. Today, the Church of England remains independent, and still has the English monarch as its head.

Queen Elizabeth II is head of the Church of England – a title that dates back to Henry VIII's reign.

During Henry's reign, England became richer. The power of the nobles and priests began to weaken, while **Parliament** and **merchants** gradually grew stronger. These changes continued in the centuries following Henry's reign.

Ruling the waves

Henry was the first English ruler to build a strong navy. He also encouraged his merchants to find new sailing routes and places to **trade**. Later British monarchs followed Henry's lead, making Britain into a powerful **seafaring** nation.

Brilliant buildings

Henry's reign was a great time for building. He improved buildings begun by his father, such as King's College Chapel in Cambridge, and he also took over projects started by Thomas Wolsey. Henry was involved in the construction of Hampton Court Palace, Christ Church College, Oxford, and Trinity College, Cambridge. These buildings survive today as a reminder of the magnificence of Henry's reign.

LEARNING FROM HENRY

Henry VIII made sure that the Tudor family kept control of the English throne. He was a powerful ruler and he also left three children to reign after him. His daughter Elizabeth ruled for 45 years and proved to be a very successful monarch. Even though Henry thought a woman couldn't rule a country, his own daughter proved him wrong.

Like her father, Queen Elizabeth I was a very strong Tudor monarch. She also shared his love of music, dancing and hunting.

A walk through the life of Henry VIII

Henry meets King Francis I of France at the Field of the Cloth of Gold

1520

Princess Mary (who later became Mary I) is born

1516

1533

Henry marries Anne Boleyn. Princess Elizabeth (who later became Elizabeth I) is born

The English defeat the Scots at the Battle of Flodden

1513

1509

Henry becomes king and marries Catherine of Aragon

1502

Henry's older brother Arthur dies. Henry becomes heir to the throne

Henry Tudor becomes King Henry VII

1491

Prince Henry (who later became Henry VIII) is born

1485

Henry marries Anne of Cleves, then Catherine Howard. Thomas Cromwell is executed

Catherine Howard is beheaded

Prince Edward (who later became Edward VI) is born. Jane Seymour dies

1540

1542

1543

Henry marries Catherine Parr

Henry declares himself head of the Church of England

1537

1545

1536

1534

The English navy drives off a French invasion and the *Mary Rose* sinks

1547

Anne Boleyn is executed. Henry marries Jane Seymour. Henry starts stripping the monasteries of their wealth

Henry dies on 28 January, aged 55. Edward VI becomes King of England

QUIZ

WHAT DO YOU KNOW ABOUT HENRY VIII?

1. How many children did Henry have?

2. How many of Henry's wives were beheaded?

3. How many brothers and sisters did Henry have?

4. Henry was married to one of his wives for 16 years – who was she?

5. Who was the first owner of Hampton Court Palace?

6. Who was Henry VIII's father?

7. Which famous artist and inventor was working in Henry's time?

Answers: 1. Three 2. Two 3. Six 4. Catherine of Aragon 5. Thomas Wolsey 6. Henry VII 7. Leonardo da Vinci

29

Cross-curricular links

Use this topic web to explore the life of Henry VIII in different areas of your curriculum.

MATHS

Try to find out the birth and death dates of Henry VIII's six wives. Who had the shortest life and who lived the longest? How many of Henry's wives did he divorce? How old was Henry's youngest wife when she died?

MUSIC

Henry loved to sing and play the harp. Find out about music in Tudor Times. You could try singing a Tudor song, such as *Greensleeves*.

ART

Look carefully at the portraits on pages 5, 13 and 17. Then try creating a Tudor portrait of your own. You could show a man, woman or child.

HENRY VIII

ENGLISH

Imagine you are at the court of King Henry VIII, and write a letter home describing the king. (You can describe Henry as a young man or when he is old.)

DESIGN AND TECHNOLOGY

Try cooking a dish from Henry VIII's time. Look on the Internet for a recipe for frumenty – a popular drink in Tudor times. Make sure an adult helps you to prepare and cook this food.

Glossary

allies Friends. Countries become allies to give each other support.

annulled To cancel or end something.

colonies Countries that are controlled by another country.

falconry Training falcons to hunt and return.

fleet A large group of ships.

gallows A structure used for hanging a person until they died.

heir Someone who will take over a title after their parent dies.

invasions To send troops to take over another country.

jousting Mock fighting between two men dressed as knights.

merchants People who exchange goods for money or other goods.

navy The ships and sailors that defend a country.

nobles People born into aristocratic or high-ranking families.

Parliament A group of people who have been elected to make the laws of a country.

Pope The head of the Roman Catholic Church.

Protestants Members of the Protestant Church.

reign To rule a country.

Renaissance A period of flourishing art and science that began in Italy in the 1350s and lasted until around 1600.

rioting Behaving in a violent way, in protest against something.

Roman Catholic To belong to the Roman Catholic Church, which is led by the Pope in Rome.

seafaring To travel by sea.

taxes Money that people have to pay to their ruler or government.

theology The study of religion.

trade The exchange of goods for money or other goods.

treason The crime of betraying your king, queen or your country.

treaty A formal agreement between two or more countries.

ulcers Open sores.

Index

Numbers in **bold** refer to photographs or illustrations.

Further Information

More books to read

Historical Stories: The Story of Henry VIII
by Geoffrey Trease (Wayland, 2008)

Historical Stories: The Story of Elizabeth I
by Geoffrey Trease (Wayland, 2008)

Tudor Life series by Liz Gogerly, Nicola
Barber and Paul Harrison (Wayland, 2009)

You Wouldn't Want to be Married to Henry VIII!
by Fiona Macdonald (Wayland, 2002)

Places to visit

- Hampton Court Palace, Surrey
- Mary Rose Museum, Portsmouth
- Tower of London, London

Useful websites

www.tudorhistory.org/henry8/
Pictures and information about Henry,
with added links to key people and places.

www.maryrose.org
A website about Henry's ship the *Mary
Rose*. Includes diagrams, pictures and
a virtual tour.

www.historyonthenet.com/Tudors/
six_wives_henry_viii.htm
Information and timelines for Henry's
six wives.